Walking Through

the

Valley of Grief

A Sermon by James C. Bivins

Foreword by Kammy Bentley

D1527539

James C. Bivins

Walking Through the Valley of Grief

A Sermon By
James C. Bivins

©2021 by James C. Bivins
Independently Published

ISBN: 9798495629486

Foreword

Much like family, we cannot pick our neighbors. But in rare instances we are blessed with a kind, insightful and delightful neighbor whose companionship we do not want to live without. For me and my family, that neighbor is James Bivins. James takes the trophy for best neighbor with his many acts of kind-heartedness and his bubbly personality.

He goes out of his way to show my son and I how much he cares. Whether it is special gift that he leaves in front of our door, taking in our garbage bins, or stopping by to see if he can take our dog Hutch on a walk with, he and his dog Abbie. James goes out of his way to show that he is there for us and that we are in his thoughts.

But the best gift I have received from James is a booklet, that he handed me one day about the loss of a loved one after he learned of my father's passing. James wrote this when his own dad passed away and he has shared his thoughts with many by sermon and this helpful booklet.

James is not only my neighbor, but he is also a successful Realtor®, an attentive son, a Christian, and a Minister. James shared, "Walking Through the Valley of Grief," during the grieving period of my own father's death. It was so helpful and made such an incredible difference in the way I dealt with my loss. Death is an occurrence that no one can escape and processing a death, or the grieving process is extremely hard for all of us. James recognizes this. I want to share his words with my siblings or others who have lost a loved one. His writings help you to understand that you can survive grief and move forward after the devastating death of a loved one.

James walks you through each step of the grieving process using scripture and lessons that he has learned that help you have faith that there is hope. I am so grateful to have had his wisdom and knowledge that he graciously shared to help me through my own sorrow and grief. This booklet is a must read for anyone who needs peace and comfort during or after the death of a loved one. It has proven to me that we can survive the grief and devastation after the death of a loved one. I told James that he needed to publish this booklet to share with as many people as possible. The most wonderful lesson I have learned in the grieving process is to know that we have not lost our loved ones forever! In Jesus name Amen. Thank you, James!

With love and blessings to all,

Kammy

Preface

When I was growing up, I used to hear adults say, "The older you get the faster and faster time goes by!" I was puzzled by this because it seemed like it took Christmas forever to get here. After Christmas, it seemed like it took summer break from school to ever get here. But Christmas after Christmas came and went, as did summer break after summer break. I found myself no longer in middle school but high school, then college, then the work force and then I started getting invitations to attend my 10 - year high school reunion, 20 - year high school reunion, 30 - year high school reunion, well you get the idea. I also remember adults saying, "There are only 2 things in this life that are certain – Death and Taxes!" As I have grown older and wiser, I have experienced the reality of many people I have known who are no longer here on earth due to death. Death is a harsh reality. Almost everyone on this planet will face the agonizing "loss" of a loved one to death and many will face the "loss" of more than one loved one throughout their life. This became very real to me between the years 1998-2005. During that short seven year span, my grandfather died, my grandmother died, my uncle died, and my father died. After my father's death in 2005, in order to deal with the pain, I immersed myself in bible study and I learned everything I could about grief. As a result of my studies, I wrote what I called a selfish sermon. That is a sermon that I need to hear. My title for this sermon was "Walking Through the Valley of Grief." I would read this sermon several times and then later on, I would pull it out and refresh my memory of what I had learned. This helped me more than anything in successfully dealing with my grief. Over time, I began to share written copies of my sermon with others who had "lost" loved ones. As time went on, I began to update and preach my sermon and I used it in an Adult Bible Class, where in just one year, we had "lost" several of our members due to death. I am always amazed at the positive response I receive from countless people who have secured a copy of my sermon, "Walking Through the Valley of Grief." Over the years, it has become my most requested sermon of all time. Looking back, I know that GOD anointed this sermon and wants it shared with others. Because of this, along with the encouragement of several people who this lesson has successfully helped deal with grief, I have felt that GOD wanted me to Publish this booklet entitled, "Walking Through the Valley of Grief," just for YOU. Yes, the lessons in this sermon are just for you if you are grieving. My sincere hope is that this lesson will gently take you by the hand and heart and successful lead you, at your own pace, through your valley of grief so that you will emerge with unspeakable joy and peace and thus be able to live the rest of your life that GOD has planned for you.

James C. Bivins

Introduction

This booklet is a sermon that discusses God's Word and the stages of grief. It is designed to help people successfully deal with grief. It is intended to be read at one sitting, and then referred to as needed while one is going through the grieving process. This booklet is for those who are grieving. This lesson can also be for those who want to gain a brief understanding of the grief process. Some of you may not need this message right now, because you may not be walking through this particular valley. Perhaps you can use it to reflect on something that happened to you previously—or save it until you need it, because the time will come in your life when you will have to "Walk Through the Valley of Grief."

This booklet is simply a sermon, it is not intended to take the place of necessary medical or phycological treatments.

First, I want to Thank the Elders, Brother Dan and most of all, GOD for allowing me to be in the pulpit this Sunday Morning. I also want to Thank You for taking time out of your busy lives to be here with us this morning. Words cannot express what an Honor and Privilege it is to Worship with you today. It is my earnest desire and prayer that this lesson will be a blessing to each and every one of you.

If some of this lesson sounds familiar to you, it is because I preached a version of this message on December 6, 2009. I originally wrote this sermon/lesson back in

2005, after my father passed away. I have updated it many times over the years. It is a lesson that may be uncomfortable to you at first, but please stay with me and I believe you will receive a major blessing of peace and comfort.

The title of my lesson this morning is:

"Walking Through the Valley of Grief."

With some holidays ahead and one just past, you may find yourself thinking about those who are no longer with us, in this life, anymore.

Yes, it is a fact, unless Jesus returns, each one of us will face the physical death of a loved one and eventually our own physical death. Every year, the news media gives an end of the year review of "famous or notable" deaths. For example, we recently lost Country Music Singer Roy Clark of Hee Haw fame at age 85. We lost Paul Allen who was co-founder of Micro-Soft. He owned several sports franchises, including the Seattle Seahawks, and he also owned more real estate in Seattle, Washington than any other person or entity. His obituary mentioned he was the 46th Wealthiest Person on the planet at the time of his death. He was only 69 years old. And, just this past week, we had a National Day of Mourning for our 41st President of the United States – George Herbert Walker Bush. You see, not even wealth, fame or accomplishments will allow you to escape physical death.

Now, even closer to home, to name a few from our own congregation, we've recently lost Raymond, Orville, Juanita, Betty, Rosie, Charles, Bobbie, Christie and if you look in our membership directory for the past 10 years, you will see many many many more names can be added to this list.

Some of you may not need this message right now, because you may not be walking through this particular valley. Perhaps you can use it to reflect on something that happened to you previously—or save it until you need it, **because the time will come in your life when you will**

"Walk Through the Valley of Grief."

James C. Bivins

Many research studies tell us the most painful death experience and the most intense grief comes from the death of a spouse and/or the death of a child and then by the death of a parent. Studies have also determined the grief that accompanies suicide is unique among any other kind of grief experience.

This morning, I want us to learn about the stages and categories of grief according to scientific research and compare these to what the Bible says about grief.

Different people's grief experiences will be as different as their own unique personalities. But

the point today is for you to understand that you *can* <u>survive grief</u> **and move forward after being devastated by the death of a loved one.**

It gives me great hope to know that the <u>Lord Jesus understands our grief</u>. The prophet Isaiah looked at the character and nature of the Messiah. In **Isaiah**

Handwritten annotations: „ how? "

53:3 *"He was a man of sorrows, and familiar with suffering and acquainted with grief."* The Bible says he bears our sorrows and we can cast our "sorrows" and cares upon him.

Let's briefly look at the life of Job, he definitely had a bad time and definitely experienced the excruciating pain of grief. Job was a wealthy man, he was blessed, but in one day, he lost almost everything. Today, we are going to see how Job responded to the bad news of the death of his loved ones.

In Job 1:1-3

¹There was a man in the land of Uz, whose name

was Job; and that man was perfect and upright, and one that feared God, and eschewed evil.

*[2]And there were born unto him **seven sons and three daughters.***

*[3]His substance also was **seven thousand sheep**, and **three thousand camels**, **and five hundred yoke of oxen**, and **five hundred***

donkeys, *and a very great household; so that this man was the greatest of all the men of the east.*

Now to:

Job 1:18-22. *[18]While he was yet speaking, there came also another, and said, Thy sons and thy daughters were eating and drinking wine in their eldest brother's house:*

[19]And, behold, there came a great wind from the wilderness, and smote the four corners of the house, **and it fell upon the young men, and they are dead;** *and I only am escaped alone to tell thee.*

[20]Then Job arose, and rent his mantle, and shaved his head, and fell down upon

the   ground,   and worshipped,

²¹And said, Naked came I out of my mother's womb, and naked shall I return thither: the LORD gave, and the LORD hath taken away; blessed be the name of the LORD.

²²In all this Job sinned not, nor charged God foolishly.

Before you rush to the false conclusion that Job did not

hurt or struggle, look at **Job 6:2**. *²Oh that my grief were thoroughly weighed, and my calamity laid in the balances together!*

³For now it would be heavier than the sand of the sea: therefore, my words are swallowed up.

Grief causes that kind of pain.

Let's talk about how all of us can **walk through the valley of grief** and not get stuck there, but come out the other side a stronger person and a better person. But you must walk through the valley, and it's not easy and it's not quick.

Here are <u>three things</u> you can do with your grief.

I. EXPRESS YOUR GRIEF

Number one. Express your grief. <u>Do not be "afraid" to express your grief.</u> There have been many studies and those who have studied it believe people pass through several stages of grief. I am reluctant to say that, because these are not automatic and they are not simple. You never find yourself saying "Oh, I'm in stage two, I need to move on to stage three now." It just does not happen that way.

It helps to realize there are stages and that **grief is a**

process. Most people have some of these emotions.

1. Shock

First is shock. Most people react with shock when they learn about the death of a loved one. Of course, this does not include those who have experienced the terminal illness of a loved one, because they actually go through a lot of these feelings *before* the actual death of their loved one. It's called "anticipatory grief."

Knowing Dad was going to die since 2015

Those who go through anticipatory grief do not have exactly the same grief process as those who learn of the unexpected death of a loved one. Those who suddenly learn often go into shock.

Many times, movies try to portray real life situations. Have you ever seen a movie scene where families are gathered in and emergency room waiting area, after an automobile accident or heart attack of a loved one? The doctor comes out and has to give the toughest news a physician ever gives, where he or she has to sit down with the family members and say, "I'm sorry your loved one has died." Many times, families express disbelief and refusal to accept the death of a loved one. Something physical happens to us that can push us into shock; it's as if your body experiences a burst of adrenaline, because you know you are going to face a lot of demands emotionally and physically over the next few days and weeks.

time in hospital

2. Then there is Numbness

A lot of people discover they are very clearheaded initially, because they know they have details to take <u>care of</u>, but soon it progresses into the second stage doctors have observed: This stage is called <u>numbness</u>. It's as if God has injected them with a spiritual or emotional <u>anesthetic that dulls and deadens</u> some of the immediate pain. C.S. Lewis wrote his classic book *A Grief Observed* after his wife, Joy, died. He wrote, *"It feels like having a mild concussion. There is sort of an invisible blanket between the world and me. I find it hard to take in what "anybody" says. Perhaps the bereaved ought to be isolated in special settlements like lepers."* It's like going to sleep at night and lying on

frustration with things people say- but I know they are only trying to help.")

your arm and cutting off the circulation and when you roll over your arm is asleep and tingly. You do not feel anything. God sometimes mercifully puts us in that numbness stage. Have you ever talked about somebody during a funeral and you notice their loved ones did not even cry and you thought they held up

Feels strange - you ask "What is wrong w/ me?"

well? It could be they are just in the numbness stage.

3. Then comes Pain and Fatigue

Number three. As soon as the adrenaline wears off, the pain and fatigue comes crashing down. It may happen soon or it may be delayed. Dr. Eric Lindemann talks about some of the physical symptoms of grief. *"You may experience pain in your chest, pain in your abdomen, a ceaseless throbbing in your head, nausea, faintness, dryness in your mouth, tightness in your throat that causes difficulty in swallowing, shortness of breath, a need to sigh, a general lack of energy and weariness not associated with physical exertion."* For those of you who've **walked through the valley of Grief,** do you remember how tired and drained you were after the funeral? It was hard to put one foot in front of the other and get out of bed. That's very common. You may almost feel like you're dying yourself, because the

Mom - so drained

physical and emotional pain comes crashing down. That's what Job was talking about when he said he was burdened more than the weight of the sands of the sea.

4. Another Stage Confusion

Stage four, confusion. People go through a variety of emotions, but at this stage, they may think they are going crazy. I have had people tell me of different things that have happened after the death of a loved one. For example: *A widow may say, I was sitting in a chair in my home and I looked up and saw my husband standing at the door. Then when I looked again, he is gone.*

The pathways in your brain saw that person who is so special to you and it runs through your mind again, it's just an illusion, you are not going crazy. I have even heard of widows who long after their husbands have died, say something like, I forgot and set a place for him to eat at the table tonight and wondered what time he was going to get home.

Sometimes people in this confusion stage often find themselves laughing uproariously and they feel guilty about the fact that they are laughing. During a time of grief, all your emotions are so much closer to the surface and that's why sometimes at a funeral you will find people laughing and then they start feeling guilty about it. Sometimes when people begin to laugh in that kind of setting, they may wonder if they're going crazy.

The Correct answer is Absolutely Not. Humans go through all kinds of "confusing" feelings during grief.

Sometimes in the confusion stage, people also experience anger and guilt. They'll be angry at the doctor or hospital or the person who was driving the other vehicle; they get angry at themselves. They may think, "If I had only talked to that person for five minutes longer." They start going through the "what ifs." If only…what if…if I could have only changed it.

There is a part where people even get angry at God. That's very normal to be angry at God, for a short while. But do not stay angry at God. Thoughts like "Of all the bums on the streets; of all the criminals in the penitentiary, God, you should have taken somebody like that instead of my loved one!" There's nothing wrong with having these thoughts, but do not give in to the temptation to follow those thoughts. I have told you this true story before about the man who lost his son storming into the preacher's office and pounding his fist on the desk and asking the preacher – where was GOD when My Son Died? The preacher stood up, looked the man straight in his eyes and said, the same place He was when we nailed His Only Begotten Son to the cross!

Sometimes we even get angry at the person who died. For example, now a young mother is left with a family to raise without her husband. She may think or say, I am so angry at my husband for leaving me in this situation. We are just looking for "targets" for our anger.

Why couldn't Dad accept my help before he died?
Then I am filled w/ compassion b/c he was such a strong man — he needed to be strong and not accept help b/c that would be a sign of weakness —

5. Stage Five is Flood of tears

People generally arrive at stage five, the flood of tears. This has a very cleansing, purifying effect. Do not judge people who do not weep or cry at a funeral. One of the lies propagated in the American public is "Real men do not cry." That is a

good to know ") [handwritten margin note]

lie. Often times we tell little boys "Be a man, do not cry." Or we even tell people at a funeral to stop crying. Go ahead and cry! It's okay. Remember in **John 11:35** *"Jesus Wept"* And why did Jesus weep. When he saw how devastated Martha was about the Death of Lazarus.

It's okay if you *do not* cry, too. Sometimes this is a **delayed reaction.** I have heard where a widow held up really well at the funeral and two months after her husband was buried; she received her bank statement, and for the first time in her life, she tried to balance her checkbook. She said, after two minutes she just burst into tears, put her head down on the desk, brushed the checkbook away and sobbed her heart out. She said, it was cleansing and purifying.

I have also heard about a man who held up well at the funeral of his wife. Six months after his wife's death, he was driving to work when one of his wife's favorite songs came on the radio. He began sobbing uncontrollably and even had to pull over. He put his head on the steering wheel and wept for 15 minutes. **That is not unusual; you are not going crazy.** Many people come to that stage. That's a good stage to come to.

<u>Grief is caused by loss and is just as normal as eating when you get hungry, and sleeping when you get tired.</u> The good news is: as you pass through this valley of Grief, you can make the turn. And after you've spent time expressing your grief, **you *can* come to a turning point.**

I feel like I will never be the same – will I come to a turning point?

So-- I. EXPRESS YOUR GRIEF

II. ACCEPT YOUR GRIEF

Number two, you can "**accept your grief.**" You are still hurting, but you know you have made a turn and things are getting a little better when you can admit to yourself that you are grieving and you can accept your grief. You need to come to a point where you can say, "I've been hurt; <u>I know I've been</u> "<u>hurt</u>," but I know I can <u>continue to live my life</u>." I *Dad would want me to go on –* heard this statement last week during the funeral services for George Herbert Walker Bush, we, who are here, are not dead; but <u>we are changed</u>

forever. You see, we have a "new normal." There may be a couple of stages during this transitional period of accepting your grief.

1. Selective memories

Number one, is the period of selective memories. You know you are making progress when you can come to a point where you can remember that person and *choose* to remember the <u>good things</u> about that person. Initially, the memories may be painful, but when you get to the point where you can choose to forget the painful memories and remember the positive, that's a good point.

Many people who suffer from Cancer or another terminal illness come to a point where the illness and maybe even the medical treatments affect a part of the brain that controls kindness, sanity and moral restraint. For the last months of their life, our loved ones may become a person we had never known before. I know of people in this stage who would use vile language to family members, say terrible things that they would never say if they were in their right mind. You have to remind yourself that it is the illness, the cancer and the medicines not your loved one.

You have to choose your memories. God will allow you to forget those painful memories of your loved one being sick, withered, bedridden, and attached to an IV and machines or how they looked after the automobile accident. God gives you the ability to choose your memories and remember the person positively.

2. Redirection of life

Another stage people come to is redirection of life. That involves the word H-O-P-E. Some of you may be struggling with an **incomplete grief experience.** If you're struggling with grief, your life will never again be the same. Your life has been changed because of the death of your loved one, so you must come to the point where you accept the fact and "redirect" your life knowing that person is no longer physically present with you. Do not get stuck in your grief process.

Suddenly food will begin to taste good again; you can "sleep all night" and you're looking forward to life. That's hope. In **1 Thessalonians 4:13**, Paul says, *"I don't want you to sorrow as others who had no hope,"* meaning we as Christians have "hope"; we have hope-certainty that we will be with Jesus. We have hope that we will see our loved ones again and we have hope that heaven really is a wonderful place. You are accepting your grief when you come to that point.

But there are some danger signs and I've known some people who have had incomplete, abnormal, unhealthy grief experiences. They struggled far too long with grief. There are three dangers you need to avoid in your grief process according to Medical Studies concerning grief.

(1) Denial

Number one is denial. Some people deny the fact their loved one is gone. It can be as bizarre as a woman in Buffalo, New York, who literally tried to preserved the body of her mother for years. She kept her mother's body in a freezer and would rub lotion on it trying to preserve it. It can also manifest itself in the form of making a shrine out of the bedroom of someone that has been gone for many years, leaving it exactly as it was the day their loved one died, often not even entering the room. Not ever wanting to sell the property where the room is located. This type of Denial prevents a healthy grief experience.

(2) Isolation

Secondly there is <u>withdrawal</u>. Once you go through grief, there is a temptation to totally isolate yourself and withdraw from normal relationships, a normal life, by constantly embracing your pain and grief. **That's a temptation you <u>must avoid</u>.** Do not try to **<u>walk through the valley of Grief alone.</u>** God

Don't try to be too strong-accept help along the way.

is there to help you.
Psalms 23: *"Yea though I walk through the valley of the shadow of death, I will fear no evil for you are with me God."* You'll find God there to "help" you and his people (your brothers and sisters in Christ) there, more than willing to help you through the grief process.

(3) Self-pity

Number three is self-pity. We've all known people who rather enjoyed the attention and embrace their pity far too long. I heard about a widow, who still maintained friendships with ladies her age, some had husbands and some did not. Twelve years after the death of her husband, she still could not bear to hear anyone else talk about their husband. Her chin would quiver and her eyes well up and fill with tears and she would say, "At least you have a husband. I don't even have a husband anymore."

Finally, she did that in the presence of one of her best friends who knew her well enough to say, honey, you need to get a life! I love my husband too, but I'm not going to continually mourn and cry for him 12 years after he's gone." The point here is---do not hold on to self-pity because you are not walking through the process of accepting your grief--- you are stuck motionless in it. **DO NOT**

GET STUCK IN THE VALLEY OF GRIEF!

So-- **I. EXPRESS YOUR GRIEF**

II. ACCEPT YOUR GRIEF then,

III. USE YOUR GRIEF

Number three. You can use your grief to <u>help someone</u> *- someday to help others in my situation*

<u>else.</u> Your tears can be the rain that waters someone

else's garden and if you'll use the grief process and sorrow you have been through, it can make you a stronger person and you will be well equipped to help other people. Listen to this poem based on one by Robert Browning Hamilton...

I walked a mile with laughter

She chatted all the <u>way</u>

But I was none the wiser

For all she had to <u>say</u>.

But I walked a mile with sorrow

And not a word said <u>she,</u>

But oh the things I learned

When sorrow walked with <u>me</u>.

No one enjoys grief, but once you go through the grief experience, you're

equipped to help someone
else who is grieving.

The turning point in this whole grief process for Job is found in **Job 42:10** (remember it all started way back in Chapter 1) Let's see how and when Job made the transition from expressing and accepting his grief to the point he could use his experience to help others. **This happens when you stop focusing on your own pain and loss and focus on someone else's pain.** In this whole Grief process, God revealed his power and love for Job and Job came to the point where he stopped grieving and turned to his friends and prayed for them, **he's**

not there yet - I pray to get there someday.

helping someone else.
Let's read Job 42:10:
10 And the LORD turned the captivity of Job, **when he prayed for his friends***: also the* **LORD gave Job twice** *as much as he had before.* "After Job prayed for his friends, the Lord made him prosperous again and gave him

TWICE as much as he had before."

(You are about to learn something very interesting!)

Let's Review parts of **Job Chapter 1:1-3** (get out you pencil and paper or calculator…for this)

¹There was a man in the land of Uz, whose name was Job; and that man was perfect and upright, and one that feared God, and eschewed evil.

²And there were born unto him **seven sons and three daughters.**

³His substance also was **seven thousand sheep,** *and* **three thousand camels, and five hundred yoke of oxen,** *and* **five hundred donkeys,** *and a very great* *household; so that this man was the greatest of all the men of the east.*

Look at the numbers…
Now look at **Job 42:12-13**

*[12]So the LORD blessed the latter end of Job more than his beginning: for he had **fourteen thousand sheep**, and **six thousand camels**, and a **thousand yoke of***

oxen, and a thousand donkeys.

[13]He had also seven sons and three daughters.

So, before, Job had 7000 sheep, now 14,000 sheep

Job had 3000 camels, now 6000 camels

Job had 500 yoke of oxen, now 1000 yoke of oxen

Job had 500 donkeys, now 1000 donkeys,

So far, all exactly doubled…then we see,

Job had 10 children, now has 10 children ???

Okay what is wrong with our math?

He had 10 children; God blessed him with twice as many. How many did God give him? 20? No. He gave him 10. WHY??? **This is the most <u>IMPORTANT</u> part of the Lesson...** The Crux of the lesson if you will...

<u>God only gave Job 10 new children Because Job never lost his original ten children.</u> <u>His ten children that physically died, simply transitioned</u>

from their physical state to the spiritual world. They are alive and well and waiting to see Job again when he makes that same transition. Somebody shout, Praise GOD, Amen!

Those of you who have had children, or loved ones who have died physically, but they knew the Lord, you <u>have not lost them forever</u>; they are in the Spiritual World right now <u>waiting to see you again</u>. You come to the point in your grief process where you take what you've learned and help someone else.

Dad! I can't wait to live eternally w/ you in Heaven ♥

CONCLUSION

A widow wrote a letter to her husband who died. "What it's like to be your widow is being devastated by the seemingly simple act of discarding your toothbrush. It's sorting through your clothing and wrapping the empty sleeves of a sport coat around me, sobbing into its lifeless shoulders. It's returning to familiar or favorite places that first time without you and feeling so alone. It's missing the lingering smell of your shaving lotion after a goodbye kiss. It's eating alone at a restaurant, because no one remembered that I was alone. It's sitting alone at weddings and being especially touched by 'till death do us part.' It's struggling to keep my composure seeing your empty place at the dinner table, especially on your birthday, our anniversary, and holidays. It's not finding comforting arms when I rushed home hurt and bruised by a conflict or a bad day. It's not hearing,

'Honey, I love you,' or 'You really look good in that dress.'

But I am okay, knowing that even if you could come back, you would not, not after being with the Lord Jesus Christ, nor would I ask you to trade the company of the altogether lovely one for that of an imperfect wife. But oh, how I do miss you for now."

You can walk through the valley of grief and come to the place where you say, "God, you know how much I miss my loved one, but I thank you that you're taking good care of them." Our hearts get broken. That's why Jesus said, "The Spirit of the Lord has anointed me that I might heal the brokenhearted."

The book of Isiah 61:1 reads:

The Spirit of the Lord GOD is   upon me; because the LORD hath an ointed me to preach good tidings unto the meek; he hath   sent me to   bind up the brokenhearted,   to proclaim   liberty to the captives,

and the opening of the pris

on   to them   that   are

bound; ...

And, Luke 4:18 reads:

The Spirit of the Lord is

upon me,   because   he

hath anointed me to

preach the gospel

to the poor;   he   hath

sent me to

heal the brokenhearted, to

preach deliverance to the captives, and recovering of sight to the blind, to set at liberty them that are bruised,...

If your heart has been broken by grief, I suggest you take every broken piece and offer them to Jesus right now and say,

"<u>Jesus, heal my broken</u> <u>heart and heal my "pain</u>."

You know there is a song, about a loved one who has passed on – the loved one says "If you could see me now, you wouldn't cry."

The invitation is yours, if you have any needs, Please come now as together we stand and sing!

I trust this has helped you understand and deal with your grief. I have included a brief outline below, of my sermon, for your reference.

OUTLINE

I. EXPRESS YOUR GRIEF

1. Shock

2. Numbness

3. Pain and fatigue

4. Confusion

5. Flood of tears

II. ACCEPT YOUR GRIEF

1. Selective memories

2. Redirection of life

Barriers to acceptance

(1) Denial

(2) Isolation

(3) Self-pity

III. USE YOUR GRIEF

Made in the USA
Monee, IL
10 April 2022

94485536R00059